MW01534304

Great Commission
Disciple Making
Workbook

Personal & Discovery Group Exercises

JAMES A LILLY

Copyright © March 2016 James A Lilly

Great Commission Disciple Making Workbook
Personal & Group Discovery Exercises
by James A Lilly

Printed in the United States of America

ISBN 9781498464475

The author guarantees all contents are original and do not infringe upon the legal rights of any other person or work. The views expressed in this book are not necessarily those of the publisher.

This work is made available under a Creative Commons Attribution-Share Alike 4.0 License (http://creativecommons.org/licenses/by-sa/4.0)

This work may be copied, translated, and modified, as long as all modifications and translations are made available to others under the same license. Copies of modifications and translations should be sent to jimlilly@yahoo.com.

Unless otherwise indicated, Scripture quotations are taken from English Standard Version, © 2001 by Crossway

www.xulonpress.com

Forward

This workbook contains all of the personal and small group exercises in *Great Commission Disciple Making.* It is designed to be used for small group Discovery Studies of fifteen passages. These passages lay out the components of Disciple Making that are essential to fulfilling the Great Commission. Discovery Studies are inductive studies and include the additional components of: memorizing the passages, applying them in practical ways to our lives, and telling other people what we have learned. It is these three additional steps that turn the inductive study into a Disciple-Making Process that is capable of fulfilling Matthew 28:16-20.

The following exercises are intended to challenge you to think and ask God what he wants you to learn and do. The trap to avoid is approaching them as lessons to be completed so you can move on to something else. As you reflect on them, ask yourself how you can align your life with what you are discovering. Obeying what Jesus and the Holy Spirit reveal to you and conforming your life to it are two of the disciplines of a disciple and also part of the repentance that Jesus called us to, in order to enter the kingdom of God.

If you have questions or would like assistance, please contact the author Jim Lilly, at jimlilly@yahoo.com.

Contents

STUDY GUIDE FOR DISCIPLE-MAKING TRAINING

The ideal group size is four to eight people, but as a minimum a group of two people is sufficient. For a group of six people plan on spending one and one-half hours together. The meeting times will follow the format laid out in Discovery Group Process outline on page 11.

Discovery Studies: Discovering Disciple-Making

Following is the list of Discovery Studies and the chapter in *Great Commission Disciple Making* where each is found. The other columns give chapters which are recommended and training videos that you can download.

Scripture	Description	GCDM	MM	CDM	CD	Video
Luke 10:1-11	Introduction	Intro-1,2,3	Intro-2	3, 8	1, 2	2a,3,5a,7
Luke 10:1-11	Disciple-Making Process	4	6	11, 15	15	5b, 6
John 14:15–27	Obedience	5	-	7	3, 11	5c, 8
John 1:35-51	"Come and See"	6	-	-	-	5d
Matthew 23:8–11	Our Role: "Be Brothers"	-	-	-	-	-
Deut. 6:1-15	Heart of discipleship	7	-	11	13	5e
Luke 11:1-13	Focused prayer	8	3	12	-	9
Matt. 9:35-10:16	Discipling Believers	9	5	13	-	-
Acts 16:25-34	Person of Peace	-	-	14	-	10
Matthew 28:1-10; 16-20	Great Commission	10	-	10, 17	15	12b
Matthew 16:13-21	Church Foundation	-	-	18	-	-
Discussion	Cultural Adaption	11	10	5, 6		13
Philippians 2:5-8	Culture: Jesus Model	12	-	2, 16	6	11, 5f
1 Cor. 9:19-23	Culture: Philosophy	-	-	-	-	-
Acts 17:22-27	Culture: Application	-	-	-	-	-
2 Tim. 2:1-7; 14-16	Replication: Concern	13	7	-	-	12a & c
John 15:1-11	Fruitfulness	-	-	-	-	1, 2c

GCDM — Chapter in *Great Commission Disciple Making*, Lilly
MM — Chapter in *Miraculous Movement*, Trousdale
CDM— Chapter in *Contagious Disciple-Making,* Watson
CD — Chapter in *Are you a Christian or a Disciple?* Gross
Video —Training Video URLs are on the last page of this workbook.

Kingdom is Encompassing:

(Reference in *Great Commission Disciple Making*: Chapter 1)

The Kingdom is the central message of the gospel. John the Baptist came proclaiming "repent for the Kingdom of Heaven is at hand." After he was arrested (Mark 1:14-15), Jesus took up the same proclamation. Jesus did not come proclaiming salvation, Christianity, the church, or happiness. He followed John the Baptist's message, "Repent for the Kingdom of God, or the Kingdom of Heaven, is near, or at hand" (Matthew 4:17, Mark 1:14-15). This is the central truth of Jesus' message. The Kingdom is bigger than any of these while including them all: salvation, the church, happiness and persecution besides.

Kingdom Circles — An Illustration of Cultures and Traditions

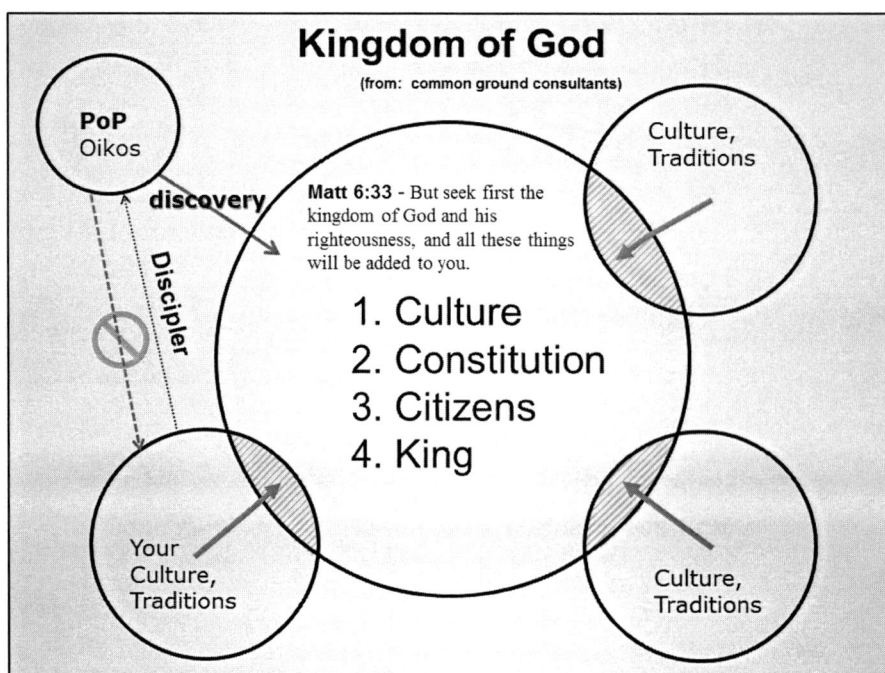

PoP — Person of Peace (Luke 10:5-6); the laborer prayed for in Luke 10:2.
Oikos — Greek word for household; PoP's social network; harvest field; Gentiles in Acts 15.

-⊘-➤ Do not bring the PoP or his Oikos into your church, or culture (Acts 15:19).

Discipler - - Disciple Maker who coaches the person of peace to facilitate a discovery study

━━━➤ The discovery process allows this Oikos to modify their existing culture to bring it into the kingdom of God according to what they learn from the Bible (Revelations 7:9).

Figure 1.1 — Kingdom Circles *(adapted from Common Ground Consultants)*

The things inside the Kingdom Circle are the unique parts of your culture that form your identity and are compatible with, but are not explicitly mentioned in the Bible. These include all your additions to the Biblical model of simple church. Things outside the circle are those parts of a culture that need to change before they can be incorporated into the kingdom of God.

2

** Personal Written Assignment 1: Kingdom Circles

When Jesus sent out his disciples, he expected them to understand and be able to proclaim that the Kingdom of God was at hand (Luke 10:11). Therefore understanding this diagram and what it represents is extremely important in the Disciple-Making Process.

Take some time to answer:

Who is the king? (1Corinthians 15:20-28)

Who are the citizens? (Ephesians 2:19)

What is the constitution? (Luke 5:1, 11:28)

What are some of the characteristics of the culture (Romans 14:17; 1Corinthians 4:20, all of Jesus' kingdom of God parables)?

The Kingdom Circles illustration of Figure 1.1 was derived from the account in Acts 15 of the First Council of Jerusalem.

Read: Acts 15:1-20 (5-19) and then answer the questions that follow.

But some believers who belonged to the party of the Pharisees rose up and said, "It is necessary to circumcise them and to order them to keep the law of Moses."

The apostles and the elders were gathered together to consider this matter. And after there had been much debate, Peter stood up and said to them, "Brothers, you know that in the early days God made a choice among you, that by my mouth the Gentiles should hear the word of the gospel and believe. And God, who knows the heart, bore witness to them, by giving them the Holy Spirit just as he did to us, and he made no distinction between us and them, having cleansed their hearts by faith. Now, therefore, why are you putting God to the test by placing a yoke on the neck of the disciples that neither our fathers nor we have been able to bear? But we believe that we will be saved through the grace of the Lord Jesus, just as they will. . . ."

Therefore my judgment is that we should not trouble those of the Gentiles who turn to God,"

Sketch of Kingdom Circles

Based on this text draw your own version of the Kingdom Circles below and write an explanation of what the Kingdom of God is, using the example of the Jews and the Gentiles. Then add circles for the groups of people that you would like to reach out to (friends, family, neighbors, coworkers, ethnic communities, etc.).

Written Explanation of Acts 15 in Reference to Kingdom Circles

Written Explanation that you would tell a Potential Person of Peace

Supplemental Reading

Great Commission Disciple Making Ch. 1 and 2, James Lilly

Miraculous Movements, by Jerry Trousdale, Ch. 6 — "Discovery Bible Studies and Obedience-Based Discipleship"

Contagious Disciple-Making, David L. and Paul D. Watson, Ch. 15 — "Discovery Groups"

** Personal Written Assignment 2: Start with Prayer
(Reference in *Great Commission Disciple Making*: Chapter 2)

The source of everything that a disciple does should flow from prayer.

First, ask God to identify what group or groups of people he wants you to reach out to. This can be any group. For example, it might be the neighbors around your church or your home, coworkers or fellow students, an ethnic group of people in your city, students at a school or university, family or church members, or activity groups or clubs, such as: bridge, skateboarders, or bowling league. There is no limit to the number of harvest fields.

In the chart below write the names of one or more groups for whom God is giving you a heart and desire to reach (See Figure 2.1 in *Great Commission Disciple Making*). Next, think of people who may share an interest in reaching any of these groups that you can invite to participate with you in the process of making disciples. They could be people inside or outside the group you want to reach. Write their names in a list beneath each of the people groups. Take time in prayer to ask God to direct you as to how and when you should invite them to join you.

Outreach Group:	Outreach Group:
Name of those partnering with you: Phone or email	Name of those partnering with you: Phone or email

Chart 1.

** Personal Written Assignment 3: Great Commission
(Reference in *Great Commission Disciple Making*: Chapter 2)

The usual approach to presenting the Great Commission is to look only at Matthew 28:18-20. But the story begins earlier in verse 16. These two additional verses give some valuable insight.

> *[16]Now the eleven disciples went to Galilee, to the mountain to which Jesus had directed them. [17]And when they saw him they worshiped him, but some doubted. [18]And Jesus came and said to them, [19]"All authority in heaven and on earth has been given to me. [19]Go therefore and make disciples of all nations, baptizing them in the name of the Father and of the Son and of the Holy Spirit, [20]teaching them to observe all that I have commanded you. And behold, I am with you always, to the end of the age."* (ESV)

In verse 16 take time to identify who went and why they went?

Who?

Why?

To whom is the command and directions in verses 18 through 20 given? What does this mean to us today; what kind of relationship with Jesus is necessary for us to be able to fulfill the Great Commission?

In verse 17 what was the response of the eleven?

What are your doubts about your role in the Great Commission?

What do we learn about the interaction of obedience, doubting, and being disciples from this passage?

What possible things can we learn from Jesus' response in verse 18 to the eleven's actions?

In verse 19 most Bibles translate the past aorist participle Greek verb (πορευθέντες — poreuthentes) as a command "go" making a separate command from "make disciples." In the Greek, the participle is literally "having gone." While there is a strong imperative connection with the two verbs, the fact is that there is only one command "make disciples" in this sentence. Translating the passage as "Therefore *having gone*, or *as you go*, make disciples, baptizing them in the name of the Father and of the Son and of the Holy Spirit," will lead to different actions.

If you understand verse 19 to be one command, "as you go make disciples," instead of two, "go and make disciples," what would you do differently?

In verse 19, who is to baptize new disciples?

What does this mean for you as a disciple maker?

In verse 20, the Greek word translated "observe" is "Τηρεῖν" (terein) which means to continue to obey orders or commands, to obey, or to be keeping commandments. In practical terms, how will teaching disciples <u>to obey</u> all that Jesus commanded differ from teaching <u>what</u> he commanded?

Jesus makes a promise in verse 20, what is it?

How have you or might you, experience the fulfillment of this promise?

From the entire passage, what are the conditions needed for the promise of Jesus' presence to be fulfilled?

** Personal Written Assignment 4: Jesus' Instructions

(Reference in *Great Commission Disciple Making*: Chapter 2)

Disciplines of Jesus' Disciples:

The five critical disciplines of a first century disciple of Jesus were:

Obey Jesus in everything.

If you love me, you will keep my commandments."
— John 14:15

Teaching them to [obey] all that I have commanded you." *My edit from the Greek.
— Matthew 28:20a

Know from Memory all Jesus' commands and teachings so they can tell others.

Have you understood all these things?" They said to him, "Yes." And he said to them, "Therefore every scribe who has been trained for the kingdom of heaven is like a master of a house, who brings out of his treasure what is new *and what is old.* (My emphasis)
— Matthew 13:51–52

Know Old Testament and learn and accept Jesus' understanding of it.

You have heard that it was said to those of old, 'You shall not murder; and whoever murders will be liable to judgment.' But I say to you that everyone who is angry with his brother will be liable to judgment; whoever insults his brother will be liable to the council; and whoever says, 'You fool!' will be liable to the hell of fire. (My emphasis)
— Matthew 5:21–22

For the kingdom of heaven is like a master of a house, who brings out of his treasure what is new and what is old. (My emphasis)
— Matthew 13:51–52

Conform their life to that of Jesus in everything (thoughts, dress, actions, speech, etc.) Jesus mission to reconcile the world becomes our mission (2 Corinthians 5:18)

A disciple is not above his teacher, nor a servant above his master. It is enough for the disciple to be like his teacher, and the servant like his master.
—Mt 10:24–25a

Do not be conformed to this world, but be transformed by the renewal of your mind, that by testing you may discern what is the will of God, what is good and acceptable and perfect.
— Romans 12:2

Make disciples after model of Jesus. This is Jesus' final command

Therefore [having gone] make disciples of all nations... Baptizing... teaching them to [obey] all that I have commanded you, and behold, I am with you always, to the end of the age."
— Mt 28:19–20

Jesus gave us a couple of qualifiers that other rabbis could not. These are extremely important in the Discovery Disciple-Making Process.

And behold, I am with you always, to the end of the age.

—Matthew 28:20b

For he has said, "I will never leave you nor forsake you.
— Hebrews 13:5b

For where two or three are gathered in my name, there am I among them.
— Matthew 18:20

But the Helper, the Holy Spirit, whom the Father will send in my name, he will teach you all things and bring to your remembrance all that I have said to you.
— John 14:26-27

But you are not to be called rabbi, for you have one teacher, and you are all brothers. And call no man your father on earth, for you have one Father, who is in heaven. Neither be called instructors, for you have one instructor, the Christ. The greatest among you shall be your servant.
— Matthew 23:8–11

Who is to do the discipling (teaching)? Who is to be our teacher?

As a disciple maker, what is your role in the discipleship process?

Based on these five sets of scriptural examples from Obey to Make Disciples, what would the Disciple-Making Process look like? Use your imagination to design a process.

Supplemental Reading
Great Commission Disciple Making Ch.3, James Lilly

Written Discovery Study

(Reference in *Great Commission Disciple Making*: Chapter 3)

In preparation for each Discovery Group meeting, each participant who is able should prepare by doing a written study of the passage that the group will study. The illustration below is supposed to represent two facing pages in a notebook. It will be helpful if you number each pair of pages and then put an index on the first page of the notebook. This will enable you to quickly find studies you have completed.

Four-Column Written Discovery Study			
First Page		**Second Page** (Page #)	
Passage from the Bible As Written	**In Your Own Words**	**Application** I will. . . . We will. . . . **Sharing Plan** • Who will you tell? • When? • Where? • How?	**Our Discovery:** • About God/Jesus • About man **Helping Plan** • Who needs help? • What help is needed? What can be done?

Figure 3.1

Using a notebook, open two facing sheets and fold each sheet to make two columns. *(The columns can be in any order desired.)*

• In each of the columns in sequence:

◊ **Column 1: Passage:** Write the passage as written — or commit it to memory.

◊ **Column 2: Your words:** Write the passage in your own words so you can tell others.

◊ **Column 3:**

▪ **Application:** Decide what you will do to apply it to your life. "I will . . ."
(Should be able to start it within 24 to 48 hours and be able to report progress by the next meeting.)

▪ **Sharing:** Plan with whom, when, and how you may share this passage. *(Should be doable within a week.)*

▪ **Helping**: What friend, neighbor, family member needs practical help.
(To suggest to your discovery group)

◊ **Column 4 Discovery:** *(Leave space to add comments from discovery group members)* Write what you learn from it about God, and man.

10

Discovery Group Process
(Reference in *Great Commission Disciple Making*: Appendix 5)

These are the five parts of the Discovery process to use when your group meets. The facilitator guides participants by asking each of the questions. See Chapter 4 of *Great Commission Disciple Making* for an explanation of the facilitator's responsibilities.

1) COMMUNITY— Opening Questions:
• What are you thankful for this week?

• What problems have you had this week?*(Counseling should take place outside group time.)*

• Is there any way this group can help you? *(Help physically or pray for these.)*

2) SHARE EXPERIENCES—Review Questions: *(These start second time.)*
• With whom did you share last week's passage?

• Did you apply what you learned since our last meeting and how did it go?

• How have you experienced God since the last time that we met?

• Update on the people your group is helping.

3) DISCOVERY — Oral Bible Study: (Read, Reread, Retell, Details)
Read the passage at least twice. The second time one person can reread it while the others just listen. Then take turns trying to retell the passage in each person's words covering all of the main points, the group should add missing parts. The **goal** is to learn together and be able to share your paraphrase of this passage with someone outside the group by memory.

Details: Discuss the passage: Participants are required to confine their remarks to the passage being studied (no preaching or teaching or outside materials). Challenge question: "Where does it say that in this passage?"

• What happens in this scripture passage?

• What do we discover about God from it?

• What do we discover about people from it?

4) OBEDIENCE — "I Will" and "We Will" Statements must be practical and measurable in 24 to 48 hours. *(Record these for next meeting.)*
Now that the group members have discovered truths from God's Word, identify what difference this makes in each of your lives.

I will change my daily life to reflect the reality that I have learned. (I will)

• If this scripture passage is true, how does it change how we see God?

• If this is true, how does this change how we treat others?

• If it is true, how does it change what we do? (We will)

5) OUTREACH — Concluding Questions:
• What other questions do you have about this passage?

• With whom will you share this story, when, and how? *(Record these for next meeting)*

• Do you know anyone who needs help? What can this group do to help them?

For believers: Pray for needs from 1) and the people with whom you will share and help.

LAST QUESTION — When do you want to meet again?

** Personal Written Assignment 5: Review the Discovery Process
(Reference in *Great Commission Disciple Making*: Chapter 5)

Take a few minutes to review what you have learned so far:

*What are the five steps of the Discovery Process?

    1.

    2.

    3.

    4.

    5.

*Facilitating is different than leading. What do you think the role of the facilitator is? (See Chapter 4 in *Great Commission Disciple Making*.)

*What is the one rule of the discovery study? (What is and is not permitted?)

*What is the "challenge question" that everyone in the group should become comfortable saying?

*What are some of the ways that you can handle a long passage during the actual Discovery Study? (Improvise ideas.)

Discovering Disciple-Making

(Reference in *Great Commission Disciple Making*: Appendix 2)

This is the list of passages that you will be studying both personally and in your Discovery Group.

Luke 10:1-11 — Disciple-Making Process

John 14:15-27 — Obedience and the Holy Spirit

John 1:35-51 — Calling disciples

Matthew 23:8-11 — Our role in Disciple-Making

Luke 11:1-13 — Focus and persist in prayer

Deuteronomy 6:1-15 — Shemah: Disciple-Maker's Orientation

Acts 16:25-34 — People of Peace

Matthew 9:35-10:16 — Compare to Luke 10:1-11

Matthew 28:16-20 — Disciples' commission

Matthew 16:13-21 — Planting churches

Philippians 2:1-8 — Model for Paul's and our actions

1 Corinthians 9:19-23 — Cultural relevance

Acts 17:22-27 — Where to start

2 Timothy 2:1-7; 14-16 — Key to replication

John 15:1-11 — Fruitfulness, love, obedience

**1. Implementation Assignment: Introductory Discovery Group
(Reference in *Great Commission Disciple Making*: Chapter 3)

Start a Discovery Group with the people you identified earlier both to practice together and form a supportive outreach group. The purpose of this group should be to participate with you in living as, and making disciples. Look over the STUDY GUIDE FOR DISCIPLE-MAKING TRAINING on page 7.

Invite the believers whom you identified in the second personal exercise and others that you have thought of since, who may be interested in engaging and making disciples, to a one-time introductory meeting. In the meeting have them read Luke 10:1-11 out loud and then watch either the 6 or 8 minute video 2 (2a or 2b)— "Act Beyond Explanation" (Video URL links are in the Video Training Resources on page 40). Discuss how they see the principles in the Luke 10 passage being implemented in the video. Next, watch and discuss:

- Video 3 Jerry Trousdale - "What are DMMs?"
- Video 7, Dave Hunt's - "Bible Study Process"

Ask them if they are interested in meeting again. If time permits, watch Part one of Ed Gross' series on First Century Discipleship, video 5a. (An alternative to Ed's series is to watch video 4, Disciple Definition, by Richard Williams.) Otherwise start the next meeting with one of these videos (Group members can watch any of these videos on their own or the group can review them if needed).

Decide which members of this group want to meet again and if they would like to invite anyone else. Then select a time when and place where you will meet. If there will be new people you will need to decide if you want to repeat this information. For those who want to continue, ask them to do the written discovery study below.

Written Assignment:
Have those who want to meet again do a written discovery study on Luke 10:1-11 in a notebook using the four column format on page 10. As a suggestion start an index of passages you study on the first page of each person's notebook. As illustrated in Figure 3.1, have them number each of the two pages studies consecutively. This index will be helpful in the future as you look back at your notes.

Appendix 3 of *Great Commission Disciple Making* has a list of detailed questions which may be useful as you begin to examine these scripture passages. Take a few minutes to look at them and decide if they will be useful to you.

Supplemental Reading
Great Commission Disciple Making, James Lilly, Ch 4, "Applying the Discovery Process"
Miraculous Movements, by Jerry Trousdale, Ch. 6 — "Discovery Bible Studies and Obedience-Based Discipleship"
Contagious Disciple-Making, David L. and Paul D. Watson, Ch. 15 — "Discovery Groups"

2. Discovery Group Exercise: Luke 10:1-11 – Making Disciples
(Reference in *Great Commission Disciple Making*: Chapter 4)

Jesus' teaching in this passage is key to understand the Disciple-Making Process that the disciples used. When Jesus told the disciples to make disciples in all the world, the process outlined in this passage is what they would have understood to be the method.

This will be your first full Discovery Group meeting. Check to see that everyone who is able has completed at least the first two columns of the written discovery study. If you want to do the written studies during your meeting allow an additional 30 to 45 minutes.

From Video Training Resources find the URL and watch video 6, Dave Hunt's presentation on "The Discovery Group Process" and take some time to read through the process described on page 11. Discuss this video and any questions that arise about the group process. This should prepare you for your first discovery group.

Next discuss each step and read each of the questions in each section before you start answering them. Chapter 3 of *Great Commission Disciple Making* provides an in depth explanation of the process and there is a concise outline of the process in Appendix 5 of *Great Commission Disciple Making*. You can read through the "Review Questions" in the second section on page 11, but this first meeting you will not be expected to answer them. You will, however, do this section the next time you meet.

Conclude your meeting time by watching video 5b of Ed Gross' series on First Century Discipleship (URL is found on page 40).

Written Assignment:
For the next meeting have your group do a written discovery using three or four columns to study: John 14:15-27 — Obedience and the Holy Spirit, our instructor. See Appendix 3 for study questions.

Supplemental Reading
Great Commission Disciple Making Ch.5, James Lilly
Contagious Disciple-Making, David L. and Paul D. Watson, Ch. 11 — "Be a Disciple Who Makes Disciples"
Are you a Christian or a Disciple? By Ed Gross, Ch. 15 — "Follow Jesus in Making Disciples"

****3. Discovery Group Exercise: John 14:15-27**
Obedience and Our Teacher the Holy Spirit
(Reference in *Great Commission Disciple Making*: Chapter 5)

This study presents a portion of Jesus' teaching on obedience and the roles of the Holy Spirit in the Disciple-Making Process.

You should have completed a three or four column written discovery study before your group meets, unless your group has decided to take the time to write it out when you are together.

Once you have completed your written study, meet with your Discovery Group. Do the entire five-part Discovery Process, adding in the accountability and encouragement portion - the goal is to help each other obey what each person believes God wants him to do.

Start by watching and discussing the following videos which can be found using the URLs on page 40 of this workbook:

- Video 8, Jerry Trousdale - "Obedience"
- Video 5c, Ed Gross – "Follow Me"

Group actions -

- Take some time immediately during the introductory questions to give thanks to God for the things that the group members share. (This is just for groups of believers — there is no expectation that non-believers would pray or give thanks to God, until they are led by the Holy Spirit to do so.)

- Write down each problem that your group shares. If there is a practical way of helping resolve it, write that down as well. If prayer is needed write that down. Use this list to pray at the end of your time together. One of the most important things you can do is pray for the needs of the members of your discovery group throughout the week.

- The oral discovery study occurs after the group members have practiced saying the passage out loud in their own words and discussed it. Write down as many of the group's discoveries as possible. This is for each person's reference as they go back and review what God has shown them.

- Next, write down all of the "I will" and "we will" statements as well as the names of the people who each person proposes to tell what they have learned. These are the practical commitments that people make and for which each group member will give a report the next time they meet.

- The last item is to identify a "group project" for the Discovery Group to reach out beyond itself, by meeting a need of others who are not involved in the Discovery Group.

  This is an activity to help the group expand its influence. By reaching outside the group, new relationships are formed. If the Discovery Group consists of people who are not yet believers and who live in a society hostile to the gospel, this both reduces possible future hostility and increases the possibility of future multiplication. For your group of disciple makers, it should be an intentional action to begin engaging the people and groups of people you want to reach.

Written Discovery Assignment:

For the following meeting, do a written discovery-study at home on John 1:35-46 and Matthew 23:8-11 - Our role in Disciple-Making - in preparation for your next discovery group

Supplemental Reading

Great Commission Disciple Making Ch.6, James Lilly

Contagious Disciple-Making, David L. and Paul D. Watson, Ch. 7 — "Disciple-Makers Understand the Importance of Obedience"

Are you a Christian or a Disciple? By Ed Gross,
Ch. 3 — "What 'Disciple' Meant in the First Century."

**4. Discovery Group Exercise: John 1:35-46 and Matthew 23:8-11
Calling of Disciples and Our Role in the Process
(Reference in *Great Commission Disciple Making*: Chapter 6)

This will be your third Discovery Group study. Using the URLs on page 40, watch and discuss video 5d, "Fruit that Remains," from Ed Gross' *First Century Discipleship*. In your Discovery Group meeting review what you have learned so far and then complete the Discovery Process focusing on John 1:35-46 and Matthew 23:8-11. These two passages define much of our role in the Disciple-Making Process. The first role of a disciple of Jesus is to bring people to Jesus and the second is to let Jesus be the rabbi as we support one another in the process. The latter is the basis for the rule that there is no teaching or preaching allowed in a discovery group.

As before, record individual needs for prayer, group discoveries, personal and corporate "I/we will" statements and the names of people selected to share the passage with. Please remember that the people you would share these 15 passages with are believers that may be interested in starting another group and joining you when you begin engaging those people who don't have a relationship with Jesus. For engaging people who are not-yet believers, use the "Discovering God" series in Appendix 2 of *Great Commission Disciple Making*. This is the first of six series, which is also found on page 39 of this workbook.

Discussion with your group - Let's get real
Take some time to evaluate how your Discovery Group is going and if there are some changes you need to make. Is the facilitator doing a good job of asking questions to draw everyone into the sharing time? Are the members of the group following through with their "I will" statement? Are they consistently sharing what they have learned during the study time? Have you identified someone outside the group to reach out to? What can you change to be more effective? Good facilitation skills are essential for successful discovery groups (see Chapter 4 of *Great Commission Disciple Making*).

Decide what changes you want to try with the group, and then make them during the following meetings so you will have some opportunities to see how they work. Let them know that each of them will take turns facilitating the group. It is important that each person in a discovery group know how to facilitate in order to encourage multiplication of other groups.

Written Discovery Assignment:
The next two chapters focus on prayer, but prayer starts with our orientation to living in the presence of God. We will therefore start by doing a written study of **Deuteronomy 6:1-15 –** The Shemah, the Greatest Commandment - Internal spiritual life.

Supplemental Reading
Great Commission Disciple Making Ch.7, James Lilly

****5. Discovery Group Exercise: Deuteronomy 6:1-15**
A Disciple Maker's Orientation to Life
(Reference in *Great Commission Disciple Making*: Chapter 7)

Start coaching a new person to facilitate the discovery process each time you meet. At the end of your time together have the group evaluate the facilitator and give suggestions to improve. The goal is that each person will develop the skills necessary to coach others to facilitate their own discovery groups.

Begin this session by watching video 5e by Ed Gross, the "The Form" (See page 40 for the URL.) As before, record individual needs for prayer, group discoveries, personal and corporate "I/we will" statements and the names of people selected to share the passage with. Please remember that the people you would share these passages with are believers that may be interested in starting their own discovery group and then joining you when you begin engaging those people who don't have a relationship with Jesus.

Discussion with your group:
During the discovery study, explore at some depth what it might mean to apply each part of the passage to your life and the life of your family. I would recommend a verse-by-verse, phrase-by-phrase study and obedience applications (See Appendix 3 of *Great Commission Disciple Making*).

Written Discovery Assignment:
The next two chapters will be on prayer and then on finding a person of peace. We will start with **Luke 11:1-13** - Focusing and persisting in prayer. Also, complete the Community Prayer Guide on pages 31 and 32 before your next meeting.

Implementation Assignment:
Discuss with your immediate family or those who live with you, how you can begin to incorporate the Discovery Process in your life together. Try engaging people you meet by asking them what they are thankful for or some other question to engage them at a deeper interpersonal level.

Supplemental Reading
Great Commission Disciple Making Ch.8, James Lilly
Contagious Disciple-Making, David L. and Paul D. Watson, Ch. 11 — "Be a Disciple Who Makes Disciples"

Are you a Christian or a Disciple? By Ed Gross, Ch. 13 — "Following Jesus' Teaching Concerning the Old Testament"

****6. Discovery Group Exercise: Luke 11:5-10 - Prayer**

(Reference in *Great Commission Disciple Making*: Chapter 8)

Watch video 9 by Jerry Trousdale, "Prayer." The URL is found on page 40.

With your Discovery Group, complete the group process. For the scripture study do an oral study of Luke 11:5-10 (See Chapter 3 of *Great Commission Disciple Making*).

Change facilitators in your training group so that each person has an opportunity to facilitate. At the conclusion of your time together, evaluate how the facilitator did in maintaining order, involving everyone in the sharing time, and drawing out the important discovery points in the passage.

In addition to the standard discovery questions about God and man, what do you discover about prayer and the work of the Holy Spirit in this passage?

Questions
- What are some successes resulting from your own prayers in the past?

- Where can you find more time to pray? (What can you give up to find the time?)

- What can you do to better focus your prayers?

- Who can you invite to pray for Disciple-Making Movements and fulfillment of the Great Commission among the people or groups you know of?

Implementation Assignment:
Complete the Community Prayer Plan on the next page. With your Discovery Group discuss one of your community prayer plans and lead them in praying through each of the eight parts.

_____ **Community Prayer Guide –**
(Reference in *Great Commission Disciple Making*: Appendix 4)
(Developed by Andrew and Heather Hocking)

Examples include a specific neighborhood, company, ethnicity, organization, affinity group, etc.

Thank God for what He is doing in the Community — Identify what God is doing.

Continue steadfastly in prayer, being watchful in it with thanksgiving. (Col 4:2)

Pray for Laborers to Partner with You

And he said to them, "The harvest is plentiful, but the laborers are few. Therefore pray earnestly to the Lord of the harvest to send out laborers into his harvest." (Luke 10:2)

Pray for someone to join you and for God to raise up workers from the harvest.

Write down names of people who can partner with you in prayer and reaching the community:

Pray for Guidance in Reaching the Community

Ask God, and write down any insight that God gives you for reaching the community:

Pray for Open Doors to the Gospel

At the same time, pray also for us, that God may open to us a door for the word, to declare the mystery of Christ, on account of which I am in prison—that I may make it clear, which is how I ought to speak (Col 4:3-4).

Pray for natural opportunities to discuss Christ and spirituality with people in the community.

Pray for Individuals

Write down individuals that you know in community:

Pray for Persons of Peace
And if a son of peace is there, your peace will rest upon him. But if not, it will return to you. (Luke 10:6)

Persons of Peace are insiders in the community who are spiritually hungry and will share spiritual things with others. Pray that God would connect you with people of peace. Make note of the individuals that fit this description and pray for them.

Pray God would Demolish Strongholds in the Community
For though we walk in the flesh, we are not waging war according to the flesh. For the weapons of our warfare are not of the flesh but have divine power to destroy strongholds. We destroy arguments and every lofty opinion raised against the knowledge of God, and take every thought captive to obey Christ, (2 Corinthians 10:3-5)

Write down worldviews contrary to the Gospel and pray God reveals truth. Write down problems in the community and pray God brings transformation in these areas:

Pray for Multiplication Inside and Out from the Community
Write down other communities to which the Gospel can spread:

Written Discovery Assignment: Matthew 9:35-10:16 – Mission of the Twelve
The next two assignments will be about finding a person of peace. Do a written study on **Matthew 9:35-10:16**. This passage describes the mission of the Twelve to reach others to make disciples. There are a few distinctions between their assignment and that of the other Seventy-two which are worthwhile noting. We will be looking at this passage in parallel with Luke 10:1-11 to discover some of the responsibilities of the disciple maker.

Supplemental Reading:
Great Commission Disciple Making Ch.9, James Lilly
Miraculous Movements by Jerry Trousdale, Ch. 3 — "Pray the Lord of the Harvest"
Contagious Disciple Making, David L. Watson & Paul D. Watson, Ch. 12 — "Prayer"

**7. Discovery Group Exercise: Matthew 9:35 - 10:16
Difference in the Work of the Twelve and the Seventy-two
(Reference in *Great Commission Disciple Making*: Chapter 9)

Complete the five-part Discovery Process with your group. In addition to the standard questions, take some time to compare the differences between the mission of the Twelve and the Seventy-two in Luke 10:1-11 that you studied earlier.

Characteristics of a Person of Peace and Role of the Disciple Maker

Matthew 10:1-16	Luke 10:1-9
And he called to him his twelve disciples and gave them authority over unclean spirits, to cast them out, and to heal every disease and every affliction. [2] The names of the Twelve apostles are these: first, Simon, who is called Peter, and Andrew his brother; James the son of Zebedee, and John his brother; [3] Philip and Bartholomew; Thomas and Matthew the tax collector; James the son of Alphaeus, and Thaddaeus; [4] Simon the Zealot, and Judas Iscariot, who betrayed him. [5] These twelve Jesus sent out, instructing them, "Go nowhere among the Gentiles and enter no town of the Samaritans, [6] but go rather to the lost sheep of the house of Israel. [7] And proclaim as you go, saying, 'The kingdom of heaven is at hand.' [8] Heal the sick, raise the dead, cleanse lepers, cast out demons. You received without paying; give without pay. [9] Acquire no gold or silver or copper for your belts, [10] no bag for your journey, or two tunics or sandals or a staff, for the laborer deserves his food. [11] And whatever town or village you enter, find out who is worthy in it and stay there until you depart. [12] As you enter the house, greet it. [13] And if the house is worthy, let your peace come upon it, but if it is not worthy, let your peace return to you. [14] And if anyone will not receive you or listen to your words, shake off the dust from your feet when you leave that house or town. [15] Truly, I say to you, it will be more bearable on the day of judgment for the land of Sodom and Gomorrah than for that town. [16] "Behold, I am sending you out as sheep in the midst of wolves, so be wise as serpents and innocent as doves.	After this the Lord appointed Seventy-two others and sent them on ahead of him, two by two, into every town and place where he himself was about to go. [2] And he said to them, "The harvest is plentiful, but the laborers are few. Therefore pray earnestly to the Lord of the harvest to send out laborers into his harvest. [3] Go your way; behold, I am sending you out as lambs in the midst of wolves. [4] Carry no moneybag, no knapsack, no sandals, and greet no one on the road. [5] Whatever house you enter, first say, 'Peace be to this house!' [6] And if a son of peace is there, your peace will rest upon him. But if not, it will return to you. [7] And remain in the same house, eating and drinking what they provide, for the laborer deserves his wages. Do not go from house to house. [8] Whenever you enter a town and they receive you, eat what is set before you. [9] Heal the sick in it and say to them, 'The kingdom of God has come near to you.'

Discussion Questions:

- Where was each of the two groups to go? What are some clues to the destination of the Seventy-two?

- What are the common instructions of the two groups?

- Where might the Seventy-two have come from?

- Discuss one of your community prayer plans and as a group, pray for each of the eight parts for that community (See page 21).

Written Discovery Assignment: Do a written study on **Acts 16:25-34** – This passage describes the Philippian Jailer as a model of a person of peace. We can also see characteristics of a disciple-maker in the actions of Paul and Silas.

There are many examples of people of peace in the Bible: Lydia, the Samaritan woman at the well, Cornelius, Zacchaeus, even Andrew and Philip, and the thief on the cross all demonstrate traits of a person of peace. There are also stories in the Old Testament such as, Rahab, who hid the Israeli spies, and the widow from Zarephath near Sidon which are examples. Almost everyone who has responded to a call of God demonstrates some characteristics of a person of peace. From these we can begin to identify characteristics of a person of peace as well as the role that we are to play as a disciple maker.

Supplemental Reading:
There is no additional reading assignment. It is a good time to review or catch-up on your reading.

****8. Discovery Group Exercise: Acts 16:25-34 – A Person of Peace**
The Philippian Jailer

(Reference in *Great Commission Disciple Making*: Chapter 9)

Watch video 10, "People of Peace," by Dave Hunt (See page 40 for the URL). Then complete the Discovery Group Process. In addition to the basic three questions, make a list of the characteristics of the person of peace and the characteristics of disciple makers. You can also refer to the Matthew and Luke passages you studied in the last lesson. How would you apply these to your own life?

Characteristic of a Person of Peace:

Characteristics of a Disciple Maker:

Implementation Assignment:

With your discovery group, begin to discuss potential people of peace who you have identified. Now that you have a better understanding of the characteristics of people of peace, review and update your community prayer guide. For non-believers the "Discovering God" series starting with Genesis provides the best passages to learn and share.

Next, lead your Discovery Group in praying for workers. Write out a general description of the person of peace that God gives in prayer. Then ask God to lead each of you to the person of peace the following week. Before you go, be prepared; and when you are there, be aware and available to follow-up.

Written Discovery Assignments

In the next chapter we will look at two different passages that give a basic outline of the two goals of a disciple maker, to make disciples and plant churches.

- **Matthew 28:16-20** — Our commission as disciples
- **Matthew 16:13-21** — Instructions for planting churches

Supplemental Reading:

Great Commission Disciple Making Ch.10, James Lilly
Miraculous Movements by Jerry Trousdale — Ch. 5 — "Engaging Lostness"
Contagious Disciple Making, David Watson & Paul D. Watson,
- Ch. 13 — "Engage Lost People",
- Ch. 14 — "Finding a Person of Peace"

9. Discovery Group Exercise – Disciple-Making and Church Planting
(Reference in *Great Commission Disciple Making*: Chapter 10)

The goal of this study is to understand the role that disciple-making plays in establishing churches. In Chapter 1 of *Great Commission Disciple Making*, the chart "From Evangelism Toward Discovery-Based Disciple-Making" presents the focus of the Great Commission as being to go and start churches. Looking at these two passages together should allow you to discover the importance making disciples has in accomplishing this goal. The role of the disciple-maker remains as a catalysis to the process.

Watch video 12b, titled, "Preparing a Person of Peace for leadership," by Jim Yost (Video Training Resources).

9a. Matthew 28:1-10; 16-20 - Great Commission
You do not need to do a full study on the first ten verses, but read them to give context and understanding why the disciples went to Galilee. However, do complete the full discovery study of verses 16 to 20.

9b. Matthew 16:13-21 - A Disciple-Maker's Role in Building Churches

When your Discovery Group has completed this study, take some time to discuss and write what you have learned about your role in the Disciple-Making Process in Matthew 23:8-11 and John 14:24-27 and your role in planting churches. Develop a plan to reach people in fulfilling the Great Commission.

- Who "makes" disciples? (also see Personal Written Assignment 4)

- Who "builds" the church?

- What is your role in "making disciples?"

- What is your role in "building the church?"

- What resources does God give you to complete your part of "making disciples?"

- What resources does God give you for your role in "planting churches?"

It is important to understand that our partnership with Jesus and the Holy Spirit does not change as we move from making disciples to planting churches. The natural growth of a discovery group of disciples is to become a simple church. The resources and our role remain the same and are adequate for both tasks.

Implementation Assignment:
- Develop a mission statement for your Discovery Group. Then develop a short strategic plan and identify resources for achieving your mission. (A mission statement is short statement of your final goals and purpose as a group. Tactics vary, but a strategic plan sets the direction and defines the methods and resources to accomplish your mission.)

Mission:

Strategy:

Resources:

- Continue to pray for more workers and the specific needs of the people of peace you are working with as well as the needs of their own discovery group.

Supplemental Reading:
Great Commission Disciple Making Ch.11, James Lilly
Are you a Christian or a Disciple? by Edward N. Gross, Ch. 15 — "Following Jesus in Making Disciples"
Contagious Disciple Making, David Watson & Paul Watson —
- Ch. 10 — "Thinking Strategically and Tactically About Disciple-Making"
- Ch. 17 — "Leadership"
- Ch. 18 — "Mentoring"

****10. Discovery Group Exercise: Cultural adaptation**
(Reference in *Great Commission Disciple Making*: Chapter 9)

The Disciple Maker – With Whom to Start

As disciples we should desire to make disciples, but since Disciple-Making is about relationships, our initial success will depend on our current set of relationships. The following short exercise will help you evaluate what type of relationships you are working with.

Begin by listing the top 20 closest current relationships in your life.

1.	11.
2.	12.
3.	13.
4.	14.
5.	15.
6.	16.
7.	17.
8.	18.
9.	19.
10.	20.

Now go back and mark:
+ Beside those who are Christian;
– Beside those who are lost; and
? Beside those whose spiritual condition you don't know.

Evaluation:

The next step is a simple evaluation. Count the number of each of the three categories marked: **+**, **–**, and **?**

- High number of "**+**": You live in a Christian world. You can begin inviting believers to become disciples of Jesus and so multiply the number of disciple makers to reach the lost. This was the first assignment of the Twelve. However, as you build a base of disciples, your eventual goal should be to reach beyond believers to engage the lost people all around you.

- High number of "**-**": You have access to the lost. You are positioned to immediately begin engaging lost people. Remember to make sure you have a supportive team. Jesus sent the disciples out two-by-two. This is not meant to be a project for lone-ranger disciples. This was the assignment of the Seventy-two.

- High number of "**?**": Start sharing some of the passages you have been learning with people and ask what they think about them. You will quickly find out what these people's relationships are with God. Their answers may lead you to people of peace.

As a group: watch video 13, "Cultural Awareness," by Richard Williams, then discuss:

- What are your experiences with different cultures? Are there any ideas or general principles that you can draw from them? How could you apply them in the future?

- How can you separate the gospel from aspects of your culture such as when, where, and how you worship, how you pray, clothing, family identity, individual identity?

- Who can coach you in reaching into a different culture? Often the person of peace can fulfill this role. Even people in your own neighborhood or extended family have different social practices. Ask about: how people celebrate birthdays and holidays, who are the family or organizational authorities, how they govern, and the work ethic of the family. These questions can both help you understand the people you are trying to reach and build your relationship with the person of peace.

- What are some of your cultural additions (music, order of service, etc.) to the Bible's model of the church? Are any of these essential?

- As a group, make a list of the absolute essentials for a church to function. Think through what you can recall from the Bible, if possible give references.

Essential Elements of a Church:

Written Discovery Assignments

In the next chapter we will look at what skills a disciple maker needs in a new culture and the model that Paul of Tarsus used. Do written Discovery Studies on the following three short passages.

Philippians 2:1-5 — Paul's model for cultural flexibility — how did this influence Paul's approach to cultures? How does this demonstrate Paul's application of what he learned as a disciple of Jesus?

I Corinthians 9:19-23. — Paul's orientation to different cultures

Acts 17:22-27 — Example of Paul's transcultural practice — What do you learn about Paul's contextualization and the proclamation of the truth?

Supplemental Reading:

Great Commission Disciple Making Ch.12, James Lilly

Miraculous Movements, by Jerry Trousdale: Ch. 10 — "The Hardest People Yield the Greatest Results"

Contagious Disciple-Making, David L. and Paul D. Watson:

- Ch. 5 — "Disciple makers Realize the Structure of the Community Determines the Strategy Used to Make Disciples", and
- Ch. 6 — "Disciple makers Realize Their Culture and Religious Experience Can Negatively Influence Their Disciple-Making Unless They Are Very Careful"

**11. Discovery Group Exercises – Cultural Adaptation
Model, Philosophy, and Example
(Reference in *Great Commission Disciple Making*: Chapter 12)

Using the URLs on page 40, watch and discuss:
- Video 11, by Richard Williams - "Disciple Maker" and
- Video 5f, "Conclusion" of Ed Gross' series on First Century Discipleship.

With your discovery group, complete the entire group process using the following three passages for your discovery study. The Philippians passage not only lays out the mission and sacrifice of Jesus, but it also gives a clear picture of what Paul used as the model for his own interactions with different cultures. In the 1 Corinthians passage Paul explains his general philosophy which reflects his understanding of what Jesus modeled. The Acts passage gives a graphic example of how Paul implemented his vision for reaching the lost.

As you study these three passages, in addition to the standard three discovery questions, discuss Paul's focus on Jesus as a model. What was Paul's philosophy, and how do you see it at work in his address in the Areopagus? As the final part of the study of this passage, discuss how you can apply this to your work with the people that you are trying to reach.

11a. Philippians 2:5-8 — How did Jesus model contextualization?
Have this mind among yourselves, which is yours in Christ Jesus, who, though he was in the form of God, did not count equality with God a thing to be grasped, but emptied himself, by taking the form of a servant, being born in the likeness of men. And being found in human form, he humbled himself by becoming obedient to the point of death, even death on a cross.

- What do we learn about God and man?

- Describe the cross-cultural model that Paul saw in Jesus?

11b. I Corinthians 9:19-23 — Paul's orientation to different cultures
For though I am free from all, I have made myself a servant to all, that I might win more of them. To the Jews I became as a Jew, in order to win Jews. To those under the law I became as one under the law (though not being myself under the law) that I might win

those under the law. To those outside the law I became as one outside the law (not being outside the law of God but under the law of Christ) that I might win those outside the law. To the weak I became weak, that I might win the weak. I have become all things to all people; that by all means I might save some. I do it all for the sake of the gospel, that I may share with them in its blessings.

- What do we learn about God and man?

- Paul was a disciple of Jesus. How did he apply Jesus model in Philippians 2:5-8 to his philosophy?

- What do we learn about how a disciple models his life to conform to that of Jesus?

- What changes can you make in your own life to adopt the model of Jesus?

11c. Acts 17:22-27 — Paul Addresses the Areopagus

So Paul, standing in the midst of the Areopagus, said: "Men of Athens, I perceive that in every way you are very religious. For as I passed along and observed the objects of your worship, I found also an altar with this inscription, 'To the unknown god.' What therefore you worship as unknown, this I proclaim to you. The God who made the world and everything in it, being Lord of heaven and earth, does not live in temples made by man, nor is he served by human hands, as though he needed anything, since he himself gives to all mankind life and breath and everything. And he made from one man every nation of mankind to live on all the face of the earth, having determined allotted periods and the boundaries of their dwelling place, that they should seek God, and perhaps feel their way toward him and find him. Yet he is actually not far from each one of us,

In this passage we see one application of Paul's philosophy.

- What do we learn about God and man?

- What do we learn about how Paul researched a new culture?

- How did Paul apply what he learned?

- How did Paul balance contextualization with truth?

- How can we apply this to our own outreach?

In your Discovery Group discuss how to develop a relationship with people of peace. Then discuss how to guide them to starting their own discovery group.

Written Discovery Assignment
Complete two Discovery Studies:

2 Timothy 2:1-7; 14-16 — Key to replication
John 15:1-11 — Call to be fruitful

Look at:
Genesis 1:1-25 — How to establish a foundation

Supplemental Reading:
Great Commission Disciple Making, James Lilly, Ch.13
Miraculous Movements, Jerry Trousdale
- Ch. 7 — "Simple Churches, Dramatic Transformation, Rapid Replication"
Contagious Disciple-Making, David L. and Paul D. Watson
- Ch. 2 — "Disciple Makers Deculture, Not Contextualize, the Gospel"
- Ch. 16 — "Establish Churches"
Are you a Christian or a Disciple? by Ed Gross
  - Ch. 6 — "Jesus and Evangelism,"

12. Discovery Group Exercise: 2 Timothy 2:1-7; 14-16 - Replication

(Reference in *Great Commission Disciple Making*: Chapter 13)

Using the URLs on page 40, watch and discuss the two videos by Jim Yost: 12a, "Lack of Obedience" and 12c, "Multiplication."

Complete the discovery study on 2 Timothy 2:1-7; 14-16.

In addition to the questions about God and man, discuss how this advice to Timothy would apply to what you need to do. Read through the following passages and discuss their application to training a new facilitator as well as your own group's goals.

- Matthew 13:3-23 — Sower of seed, pathway, rocky, thorns, good ground
- Matthew 21:19 — Cursing the fig tree
- Matthew 13:31-33 — Mustard seed
- Colossians 1:6-7 — Epaphras a faithful brother
- John 1:35-51 — Come and see
- Ephesians 6:10-20 — Spiritual Armor — (This is a good addition to your own group's prayer).

Role Play:
Review the Kingdom Circles and role play explaining the Kingdom of God as Jesus' message to a potential person of peace. Draw the circles as you explain Jesus' message.

Develop your skills as a facilitator
As you conclude your own Discovery Group time, take a few minutes to discuss what you have learned about facilitating a discovery group.

The first obstacle in the Discovery Process is becoming comfortable with both the order of the process and in your ability to facilitate groups. Helping each other improve in facilitating a Discovery Group and understanding group dynamics is essential if you are going to lead a group of not-yet believers yourself or train a person of peace.

Written Assignment:
Complete a written study of John 15:1-11. The final lesson in this training series will connect obedience and fruitfulness.

**13. Discovery Group Exercise: John 15:1-11
Fruitfulness and Obedience
(Reference in *Great Commission Disciple Making*: Chapter 13)

Using the URLs on page 40, watch and discuss:
- Video 1, Cityteam, "DMM Overview" and
- Video 2c, Act Beyond, "New Movements"

The final study for your introduction to Disciple-Making is John 15:1-11, in which Jesus strongly links abiding in him with fruitfulness and obedience. Nowhere in the gospels does Jesus specifically define what he means by fruitfulness, but here it is obvious that it characterizes the life of all of his disciples. It is abundant and it abides, enduring forever.

With your group discuss what it might mean for you to be fruitful.

Engagement Partnerships
If you wish to engage a large people-group, assembling or becoming a part of team of people who engage their physical needs is best.

What other ministries or groups are working with the people you want to reach? Write names and contact information:

Establish Prayer Networks
It is of primary importance is to seek to establish prayer networks. The best people to engage in this work are people who have a burden for the particular group that you are trying to reach. Join with other groups who are working to reach the same or similar groups of people to pray regularly.

Who can you invite to begin praying for you and the people you want to reach? These can be individuals or existing prayer groups. For instance you may want to approach your church's mission board or prayer ministry. Write their names and contact information.

Starting to Reach Out
At this point you and your small group should be prepared to focus on fulfilling the Great Commission by making disciples wherever you go. When you have completed this lesson, take some time to discuss how you will implement what you have learned. Read the "Great Commission Outreach Guidelines" that follow. Schedule your next meeting to begin finding people of peace.

Written Assignment: As you begin reaching out, start with the Discovering God Scripture Series that follows and be prepared to share these passages from memory. Additional and specialized study passages can be found in *Great Commission Disciple Making's Appendices 2 and 7.*

Great Commission Outreach Guidelines

(Reference in *Great Commission Disciple Making*: Appendix 1)

Purpose: Everything you have learned so far has been to prepare you to fulfill Jesus' final command as outlined in Matthew 28:16-20. Your group's focus should now shift from preparation to implementation, from becoming disciples to making disciples, who in turn can make disciples. Just as the Apostles operated in teams, so you should continue to operate as a team.

The Discovery Process is simple, but implementing it takes commitment, prayer, work, and flexibility. As you have learned, it is a partnership with Jesus by means of his word, and the Holy Spirit. Your responsibilities are limited and well defined: pray the Lord of the Harvest to send laborers; as you go, with prayer and blessings, look for and find them; bring your person of peace to Jesus and his word where Jesus promises to be there (two or more gathered), teach him or her to teach his group to obey all that Jesus' Spirit commands them.

Goal: That you and your group will find one or more people of peace who will become the worker or workers to lead his or her family and/or social group into the kingdom of God and will in turn replicate by reaching others within their communities.

General: Plan on a minimum of 12 to 14 implementation sessions with your group of disciple makers. The meeting times and dates need to fit your schedules. I suggest meeting biweekly or monthly to give yourselves time to implement what your group decides to do. Following are only suggestions, but may give you a place to start your own planning.

First meeting: Determine the group of people you want to reach. Complete or review your "Community Prayer Guide" that you should have started during this training (See page 21 of this workbook and Appendix 4 of *Great Commission Disciple Making*). Determine what additional information you need about this group and how you will obtain it. If you have sufficient information, review the six Discovery Series in Appendix 2 of *Great Commission Disciple Making* and determine what series of scriptures would work best to engage them. Depending on the underlying belief system of the group you are trying to engage, you may need to modify the discovery passages. (In addition to the standard Discovering God series, there are some topical studies that can be used to engage people which are available in Appendix 7 of *Great Commission Disciple Making*.)

Sample Meeting Agenda:

Follow the five part Discovery Group Guide:

1. **Community: Opening questions:** In addition to focusing on your individual needs, include questions about finding people of peace and developments in the new discovery groups. This builds strong relationships with your team with a focus on your mission.

2. **Share Experiences** is the place you can report progress with reaching people of peace as well as each member's "I will" and the groups "we will" statements. If there are difficulties in finding or working with people of peace, the group can work out solutions or approaches.

3. **Discovery Bible Study** should have two parts. The first is a review of one of the passages from the training seminar. The second is a full discovery study on one of the "Discovering God" passages (see the next page).

   With **the review passage** from the Discovering Disciple-Making series on page 11, focus on how you can implement this passage in your own lives as well as reaching others.

   With **the outreach passage**, (from the discovering God series) in addition to the normal discovery process, identify the essential elements of the passage, so that the facilitator (person of peace) of the community Discovery Group can be prepared to use questions to draw out his group members when needed. These leading questions assure that the basics in each passage will be discovered. This is especially important as the new Discovery Group starts.

4. **Obedience** is time for brain storming and to make personal commitments on how to reach your target community. Don't neglect your own growth as disciples. Develop "I will" and "we will" statements from each of the Discovering God passages you study.

5. **Outreach**, is the time to discuss your plans to share the passage you are memorizing and make plans to better connect with your outreach community. Identify the needs and ways to meet those needs is a good place to start.

Close your time with a time of prayer for the needs of your group and particularly for the needs of the community you are trying to reach.

As you continue to meet you may need to adjust the time and frequency of your meetings. Always confirm the next meeting with everyone.

Discovering God Scripture Series

(Reference in *Great Commission Disciple Making*: Appendix 2)

God Creates — Genesis 1:1-25

God Creates Man and Woman — Genesis 2:4-24

Man and Woman Eat the Fruit — Genesis 3:1-13

God's Curses — Genesis 3:14-24

God Regrets His Creation — Genesis 6:5-8

God Saves Noah and His Family — Genesis 6:9-8:14

God's Covenant with Noah — Genesis 8:15-9:17

God's Covenant with Abram — Genesis 12:1-8, 15:1-6, 17:1-7

Abraham Gives His Son as an Offering — Genesis 22:1-19

God Spares His People — Exodus 12:1-28

The Commands of God — Exodus 20:1-21

The Sin Offering — Leviticus 4:1-35

God's Righteous Servant — Isaiah 53

Jesus is Born — Luke 1:26-38, 2:1-20

Jesus is Baptized — Matthew 3; John 1:29-34

Jesus is Tested — Matthew 4:1-11

Jesus and the Religious Leader — John 3:1-21

Jesus and the Samaritan Woman — John 4:1-26, 39-42

Jesus and the Paralyzed Man — Luke 5:17-26

Jesus Calms the Storm — Mark 4:35-41

Jesus and the Man with Evil Spirits — Mark 5:1-20

Jesus Raises a Man from the Dead — John 11:1-44

Jesus Talks about His Betrayal and the Covenant — Matthew 26:17-30

Jesus is Betrayed and Faces Trial — John 18:1-19:16

Jesus is Crucified — Luke 23:32-56

Jesus is Resurrected — Luke 24:1-35

Jesus Appears to the Disciples and Ascends to Heaven — Luke 24:36-53

Enter the Kingdom of God — Acts 2:25-41

Justified by God's Grace — Ephesians 2:1-10

Video Training Resources — Current in 2016

(Reference in *Great Commission Disciple Making*: Appendix 6)

It is recommended that you download the videos listed below to use in your training.

1. Cityteam — DMM Overview (5 min.): https://www.youtube.com/watch?v=29b-KlAFr28

2. Act Beyond — Explanation

    a. Disciple-Making Training (8 min.): http://vimeo.com/84442681

    b. Awareness Training (6 min.): https://vimeo.com/76341533

    c: New Movements (14 min.): https://www.youtube.com/watch?v=2j8Y5NMSZPQ

3. Jerry Trousdale — What are DMM (3 min.): https://www.youtube.com/watch?v=6xlVhXw9G4A

4. Richard Williams — Disciple (5.5 min.): https://www.youtube.com/watch?v=JidJe9PkmOE

5. Ed Gross — First Century Discipleship

    a. Introduction (4 min): https://www.youtube.com/watch?v=qlREyeb671g

    b. Part 1: The Foundation (12 min.): https://www.youtube.com/watch?v=x_Ma5fwYaYM

    c. Part 2: Follow Me (12 min.): https://www.youtube.com/watch?v=tUY8JQ0WkKI

    d. Part 3: Fruit That Remains (13 min.): https://www.youtube.com/watch?v=ArIo9uy7W8o

    e. Part 4: The Form (13 min.): https://www.youtube.com/watch?v=HvMc3VsMNq8

    f. Conclusion (13 min.): https://www.youtube.com/watch?v=UqjIXWYJs-0

6. Dave Hunt — Group Process (4 min.): https://www.youtube.com/watch?v=dHggzCWYL-Q

7. Dave Hunt — Bible Study Process (5 min.): https://www.youtube.com/watch?v=azJq4McK7uc

8. Jerry Trousdale — Obedience (4.5 min.): https://www.youtube.com/watch?v=bvQJdKCHn2M

9. Jerry Trousdale — Prayer (4 min.) https://www.youtube.com/watch?v=hzgWV4i8tEs

10. Dave Hunt — People of peace (3 min.): https://www.youtube.com/watch?v=m_lvX5UfM3Q

11. Richard Williams — Disciple Maker (6 min.): https://www.youtube.com/watch?v=V5zA9FaLn-E

12. Jim Yost — Inhibitors to DMM

    a. Part 1: Lack of Obedience (3 min.): https://www.youtube.com/watch?v=tjgfU4XKgAw

    b. Part 2: Preparing a PoP (2 min.): https://www.youtube.com/watch?v=ia8OvFtd6Tw

    c. Part 3: Multiplication (2 min.): https://www.youtube.com/watch?v=aSdf-wD5EMg

13. Richard Williams – Cultural Awareness (6 min.)
https://www.youtube.com/watch?v=kTQwsYgstto&index=7&list=PLpwVfGF_movk8uNhudJmr9U4NEGJviD3b